How to Make Money Online

How Using Fiverr and Kindle Publishing Has Allowed Me to Quit My Job and Work Only Four Hours a Week

James Chen

How to Make Money Online © Copyright 2014 by James Chen. All rights reserved.

Published by Gamma Mouse http://gammamouse.com

This document is geared towards providing exact and reliable information in regards to the topic and issue covered. The publication is sold with the idea that the publisher is not required to render accounting, officially permitted, or otherwise, qualified services. If advice is necessary, legal or professional, a practiced individual in the profession should be ordered.

From a Declaration of Principles which was accepted and approved equally by a Committee of the American Bar Association and a Committee of Publishers and Associations.

In no way is it legal to reproduce, duplicate, or transmit any part of this document in either electronic means or in printed format. Recording of this publication is strictly prohibited and any storage of this document is not allowed unless with written permission from the publisher. All rights reserved.

The information provided herein is stated to be truthful and consistent, in that any liability, in terms of inattention or otherwise, by any usage or abuse of any policies, processes, or directions contained within is the solitary and utter responsibility of the recipient reader. Under no circumstances will any legal responsibility or blame be held against the publisher for any reparation, damages, or monetary loss due to the information herein, either directly or indirectly.

Respective authors own all copyrights not held by the publisher.

The information herein is offered for informational purposes solely, and is universal as so. The presentation of the information is without contract or any type of guarantee assurance.

The trademarks that are used are without any consent, and the publication of the trademark is without permission or backing by the trademark owner. All trademarks and brands within this book are for clarifying purposes only and are the owned by the owners themselves, not affiliated with this document.

How to Make Money on Fiverr Secrets Revealed

How Using Fiverr Has Allowed Me to Quit My Job and Work Only Four Hours a Week

James Chen

How to Make Money on Fiverr Secrets Revealed © Copyright 2014 by James Chen. All rights reserved.

First Edition: June 2014
123456789
Published by Gamma Mouse http://gammamouse.com

This document is geared towards providing exact and reliable information in regards to the topic and issue covered. The publication is sold with the idea that the publisher is not required to render accounting, officially permitted, or otherwise, qualified services. If advice is necessary, legal or professional, a practiced individual in the profession should be ordered.

From a Declaration of Principles which was accepted and approved equally by a Committee of the American Bar Association and a Committee of Publishers and Associations.

In no way is it legal to reproduce, duplicate, or transmit any part of this document in either electronic means or in printed format. Recording of this publication is strictly prohibited and any storage of this document is not allowed unless with written permission from the publisher. All rights reserved.

The information provided herein is stated to be truthful and consistent, in that any liability, in terms of inattention or otherwise, by any usage or abuse of any policies, processes, or directions contained within is the solitary and utter responsibility of the recipient reader. Under no circumstances will any legal responsibility or blame be held against the publisher for any reparation, damages, or monetary loss due to the information herein, either directly or indirectly.

Respective authors own all copyrights not held by the publisher.

The information herein is offered for informational purposes solely, and is universal as so. The presentation of the information is without contract or any type of guarantee assurance.

The trademarks that are used are without any consent, and the publication of the trademark is without permission or backing by the trademark owner. All trademarks and brands within this book are for clarifying purposes only and are the owned by the owners themselves, not affiliated with this document.

Making Money On Fiverr: The Basics

The #1 Rule for Fiverr Gigs

Money. We would all like more of it. And Fiverr is a fantastic resource for making money. A lot of money. But you have to be careful not to fall into an easy trap with Fiverr, which is undervaluing your time. Too often sellers start a gig that takes too much time to fulfill. Since you only make four dollars for each gig—with Fiverr taking the other dollar—it makes sense that your gig should not take you longer than ten minutes to complete. The shorter it takes, the better.

This rule is the most important thing to keep in mind when posting a gig. How long will it take me to do? Think about it this way: if it takes you ten minutes to complete a gig at 4 dollars per gig that is 24 dollars an hour. This should be your minimum rate. Now compare this with it taking a half hour to complete a gig. That will give you only $8 an hour. That's essentially a minimum wage job.

Let's take it a step further. Imagine you have an unlimited amount of gigs. If your ceiling is $8 per hour, no matter how hard you work, you are not going to break through. Your chances improve if you hit the $24 an hour mark, but even then you have to work constantly to make more money.

The Best Gigs

The point is that to make money on Fiverr, you can't post any type of gig; most will not make you money because you have to work too long and too hard. The best gigs are ones that can be completed easily or in which the information is complete and just needs to be sent to the buyer. In the past, I've had gigs that sold pdf documents to buyers that contained everything from recipes to dating information. It is great when it sells, but there was never much demand. While it is a good gig to have posted on Fiverr, it won't make you money. So just because you can do it quickly doesn't mean it will make you a lot of money. The demand has to be there, too.

These type of easy gigs without much demand are fine to keep up, just understand that they won't be your bread and butter. Some gigs seem easy, but can be actually quite time consuming. Video testimonials, audio transcription, singing or playing an instrument, and drawing or doing any kind of art takes way too much time and effort. Even if you are fantastic at these areas, you still need to invest the time to complete the order. And you want to be able to over-deliver on your gigs so you can get repeat customers; I don't see that happening with these types of gigs.

How to Really Make Money Using Fiverr

So this leaves us with the question: what is an acceptable gig? I will give you one type of gig that does well on Fiverr; it is actually easy to complete and has a high demand. But even that gig doesn't take advantage of Fiverr, using it to its fullest potential. In order to do that, you need to buyer and not a seller, and market your product to those outside of Fiverr. This sounds more complicated than it truly is. And I will go through it later in this guide. The reason it makes money is simple: you spend your time getting leads and customers, while a seller on Fiverr does all the work. And you end up charging much more than five dollars.

The beauty of Fiverr is using the sellers as outsourcers who are able to supply product for you. You then charge your customers much more. Think of it as being the middleman in the transaction. You buy the product on Fiverr for wholesale, and then turnaround and sell it for any price you wish; you dictate the market.

Does it work? Absolutely. The right products sell themselves. Even better, with these products it will be incredibly simple to target your audience.

Most books will tell you how to make money on Fiverr. This one will tell you how to make money using Fiverr. The difference—and potential profits—are huge.

What Makes Money on Fiverr

So we know that we want a gig that doesn't take much time to fulfill. As I mentioned earlier, sending pdf documents that cover various topics are great gigs. The demand isn't going to be high, though. So if we want to actually make a fair amount of money we need to focus on another type of gig.

Gig Extras

But first I want to talk about gig extras. These are extras you can charge customers on your gig when you become a Level 1 seller. Gig extras can definitely help you make more money from your gig. However, you never want to lose sight of how long it takes you to do the basic gig. If it is more than ten minutes, then gig extras still are not likely to help you supercharge your business. Because this book is more about using Fiverr than selling on Fiverr, gig extras will only be briefly mentioned. While they can be helpful to your bottom line, to really make money you are going to want to use Fiverr to outsource your work, while selling it for a much higher price.

Sneaky Tricks to Get Noticed

When you are first starting out on Fiverr, you won't get many views or orders for you gig. The way the system is it takes time to get orders. And complete orders and positive reviews are necessary to really see future orders. The good news is that if you are in the high-demand field I will tell you about, orders should eventually come your way after a few days. If you don't get an order within ten days, I would suggest deleting and re-posting your gig with slightly different wording.

Another suggestion is to have a friend buy your gig and post a positive review on it. This will greatly help, improving your visibility. Many customers won't even bother with your gig if you don't have at least one review, so getting that review as soon as possible is highly recommended.

Also, if you are having problems getting interest in your gig, email Fiverr asking if they can promote your gig. Fiverr support is excellent, and they have been very receptive to this in the past, so I highly recommend doing it. At the very worst, they say no, but it is always worth trying, because if they promote you, you will see a lot of orders.

Another way to get recognition quickly is to provide more than your competitors. It is a good idea to look at the gigs of your competitors, see what they are offering, and see which ones are having success. Then try to offer a little bit more. If you can highlight this difference in your gig title, even better; it will produce results. Once you have gotten a few reviews, and the orders start to pile up, you can edit your gig to be more in line with your competitors. Undercut them to get noticed, but once noticed you no longer should offer additional service.

When the orders do start to come in, make certain that you deliver them on time. Delivering orders late will have serious repercussions for your gig, so don't do it. With the gig I'll suggest this shouldn't be a problem, but understand that if you want to be successful on Fiverr you can never deliver late.

Be professional. You might be surprised at how many Fiverr sellers lack professionalism. You want to make certain that you are incredibly responsive to your potential customers; try to answer their questions as quickly as possible. Repeat customers will be your lifeblood, so you want to make sure you treat all your customers well so that they will come back. I always try to work within my customer's requirements as long as they don't violate my rule about a gig taking longer than ten minutes. Gigs that allow you to over-deliver on the product easily are great, leaving the customer believing that they got a fantastic deal. Leaving your customers happy is a great way to continue to make money with any Fiverr deal.

Start with this Money-Making Gig

That is enough of the preliminaries. I now want to look at the gig you want to set up on Fiverr. There is a huge market on Fiverr for reviewers. The most common ones are for book reviewers or product reviewers, and the most popular site for these reviews to be posted on is Amazon. You will want to set up two gigs, one for book reviewing and one for product reviews, and you want to focus on Amazon, so you will need an Amazon account to post reviews.

Most of the authors looking for book reviews want the reviews to be verified. A verified review means that you have purchased the book. Don't worry too much yet about buying the book, the customer will reimburse this expense for you.

When I set up the gig, I promise that my reviews will be up to 50 words, this is a target that I can easily hit within a couple of minutes. There is no point in competing on the word length of your reviews. I see Fiverr sellers who promise 300 word reviews; this is serious overkill. Reviews like this don't appear very organic, which is a great way to get Amazon to delete all your reviews. So keep your reviews shorter and try to make your writing appear organic—so don't overthink it.

There a few gig extras that should go with your book reviewer gig. One should be an extra where you agree to post your review on additional sites like Goodreads or Barnes & Noble. Essentially, these additional tasks should take you a couple of minutes to complete. Even at an additional $5, this gig extra has proved very popular. Another gig extra you will need to have is an extra fast option. When you start out your gig, you want to have a delivery time of around 5 to 7 days; this will help you not get too overwhelmed when the orders start flying in. This delay also helps sell your extra fast option of 1 day to buyers. Usually, I charge $10 for the extra fast option. While it is not extremely popular, people do buy it, and that is essentially free money, because it adds nothing to your workload.

The very last gig extra I use is one in which I offer a verified review option. This extra states that I will purchase their book from 99 cents to $3.99. This is another great extra that doesn't add to your workload, and though it is for purchasing the book, you end up making money on this extra. Most authors have their books priced at either 99 cents or $2.99. You get $4 for the gig extra, so you end up pocketing the difference. It's not much, but it can mean that you are making 6 or 7 dollars per gig instead of $4. You'd be surprised how quickly that can add up.

When it comes to my product review gig, I will use only the extra fast option as an extra. Don't bother offering verified reviews as paying for products and wanting for them to be shipped is a hassle. We want to keep our time expenditure short, which means posting quick reviews only without having to wait a week for an item to arrive.

Earlier, I talked about repeat customers and how they are the lifeblood for any Fiverr seller. Well, this is really true when selling reviews; a huge percentage of my orders are from repeat business. This is why it pays to be professional and responsive to your customers.

If you can get a popular review gig on Fiverr, you can make some easy money in very little time. One of my book review gigs was making just over $1000 per month, and it only took me at most forty-five minutes a day to fulfill my orders. While you wouldn't be able to quit your job, it's a nice little bonus for only working forty-five minutes a day.

But to make real money off Fiverr, we are going to have to be able to sell our products for more than five dollars.

The First Fiverr Money-Making Trick

I am now going to get into the real meat of money-making on Fiverr. Over the next three chapters, I will present three product ideas that you will sell to others, but buy on Fiverr. Each of these three ideas can be done separately, or I will show you how to put them all together to maximize your revenue.

Spend your Time Selling

To really make money using Fiverr, you need to concentrate on getting customers and outsourcing the real work to other Fiverrs. This allows you to price your product however you wish. Honestly, we need to make more than the four dollars we get for each Fiverr gig we complete. We need to find customers that will be willing to pay hundreds of dollars for things we can get for five dollars.

Doesn't that sound much more appealing? Let me tell you—it is!

You will remember from the previous chapter how I explained that book review gigs are very popular gigs to start. There is a huge audience for reviews on the Internet. Many of these people and businesses have no idea that Fiverr even exists.

Selling reviews to businesses is the crux of this method. Particularly selling businesses reviews on Yelp. You can use other review sites, but I will concentrate on a system that uses Yelp.

Here is What I Do

The first thing you need to do is get a customer list. Don't worry, it isn't as difficult as it seems. Go to Yelp and essentially go through the businesses, either on Yelp or at the respective website, and get their contact information. It is that easy.

I will then take this list and email them. I have a form letter which offers my services, namely I will provide them with a positive Yelp review for a set price. If the business responds—and you would be surprised at how many do—I will often collect half of the fee up front and the other half on delivery. To make things easier, I use Paypal to complete the transaction.

Once the order has been placed, I then go to Fiverr and hire a gig to complete the review. So if I sell the review for $20, and pay someone to write it for $5, I end up $15 ahead. Not bad, huh?

But this can be better and I will show you how when I explain how to put everything together. The most important thing you can do is build a customer list as you will be using this for all of the methods that I present. The power comes when combining the methods, taking the average package price from a $20 Yelp review to over a hundred dollars.

Making it Work for You

Once you have this general idea down, you can offer reviews for any site. For example, if you want to offer Amazon reviews, you might want to put together your contact list by visiting sites dedicated to writing and writers. Usually targeting customers to build up your list is easy because the groups are easily identifiable and can often be found on the Internet with little effort.

The Second Fiverr Money-Making Trick

The second trick I'm going to present has the same setup as the selling Yelp reviews technique. You will need a customer list of businesses, once again you can get this by researching on Yelp or any other site that provides online business listings.

A Quick Way to Supercharge your List

Honestly, I have never built my own list of contact information for businesses. I have always outsourced this job to a Virtual Assistant. You can hire one for only a few dollars per hour on an outsourcing site like Odesk (http://www.odesk.com), Elance (http://www.elance.com), and even Fiverr has individuals offering to be your Virtual Assistant for a set period of time.

I usually task the assistant with finding business email addresses through a site like Yelp, and usually within a certain city. I like to sort the email addresses to remove any duplicates which I can easily do in Excel, so I suggest having your assistant enter the email addresses in the spreadsheet. Another way of doing it is to enter it in a spreadsheet in Google Docs. For very little money, you can build a fairly comprehensive client list using Virtual Assistants, so I highly recommend it. This will save you time to concentrate on your other ventures.

Putting the Second Trick into Action

The second item we are going to offer to our client list is social media proof. This can be Facebook page likes, Twitter followers or re-tweets, maybe Instagram or Youtube likes. Essentially, we can offer a huge range of social media proof.

There are quite a few sellers that sell real Twitter followers or Facebook likes on Fiverr. Usually they will offer hundreds for five dollars. This is a great place to buy these when you do make a sale.

Be aware that you can also provide the same results by using a social media exchange like Like4Like (http://www.like4like.org). The way a social media exchange works is that you earn credits by liking other people's pages, and then spend those credits when people like your page. You can also pay for credits which might be the easiest method to take depending on how much you are selling the "likes" to your client for.

Understand that when you buy a gig on Fiverr that will give you hundreds of "likes" that these individuals are using a social media service like like4like.org. I want you to know this so you can outsource the job appropriately.

Another option would be to hire a Virtual Assistant to earn the credits through the social media exchange. Whether this is a better solution than paying for the credits either outright or through a Fiverr seller will depend on how much the assistant charges per hour and how many credits they can earn during that time.

To find the method that works best for you will require some experimentation. You may find a great gig on Fiverr that handles everything perfectly. Or you may find that buying the credits saves you the most money and time in the long run. I just wanted to present you with a few different options to help you find the best solution.

How Much Should I Charge?

I have charged some businesses as much as a dollar per "like". However, I suggest over-delivering, if possible. If you can provide 200 "likes" for $50, you will likely have a lot of happy clients. If the demand is high for this package, fiddle with the numbers, just as if the response is tepid, try offering more. Knowing your target is also helpful. Small businesses have less money to spend on this type of marketing, so they will be looking for more bang for their buck. More established businesses may be willing to spend a lot more, however they might be harder to reach someone who can make that decision. The small Mom-and-Pop type businesses are the ones that often gravitate to the services that I offer. This is a good thing to keep in mind when you are deciding on your pricing.

The Third Fiverr Money-Making Trick

The third trick I am going to present once again uses the same setup of the previous two tricks. We are going to use our client list and email them a specific service. In this case, video testimonials.

One of the great gigs that you can buy on Fiverr are video testimonials, with many of them professionally done with ultra-high quality. It is these type of gigs that we are going to want to use.

All of these testimonial gigs will require a script. The best option is to get the business you are doing the testimonial for to write it. But a second option is to outsource the script on Fiverr. You could also obviously write it yourself, but my motto is "never do yourself what you could outsource".

Video testimonials may not be as popular as the other services that you can offer, but they do have one great thing going for them: you can charge quite a bit for them. Especially if they look incredibly professional. And this is why it is important to pick a Fiverr seller who can deliver high definition quality. Because the more professional it looks, the more you can charge your client.

Businesses are convinced that video marketing is expensive, so I play on this fact. Often I will offer a video testimonial for $50 claiming it is deeply discounted. It works.

Another option is to offer to not only provide a video testimonial, but to offer posting it on Youtube and getting it a set amount of views or "likes". Once again, we can accomplish this social media proofing by using a social media exchange or Fiverr seller. This also hints at how we want to put all of these three techniques together. There is a reason we can use all these techniques on a single client list.

What Should I Charge?

I find that offering video testimonials cheaply works extremely well. As I mentioned, people assume that producing video is expensive, so it is fairly easy to offer what most people would consider an inexpensive package. Offering additional views and "likes" for the video also helps tremendously with my sales.

Pricing is one of the factors you really need to play with. I keep track of my conversions and sales for my different pricing levels to see what works best for me. And this is the point: what works best for me might not be what is best for you. How much you can earn is highly dependent on your list. Some lists will outperform others, some will earn more. It is your job to find out what prices work best for your list.

That said, offering video testimonials in the $50 range has always gotten me good responses. Even if you want to offer testimonials for $20, after you pay for the Fiverr gig you still earn $15. Which isn't too bad for being a middleman.

Which Customers Are a Goldmine?

Another thing I would like to point out: treat all your clients with respect and professionalism. It will benefit you in both the short and long run. Repeat customers are an absolute goldmine, so do everything in your power to make certain that all your clients are deliriously happy with the results you provide.

Also, as you get clients make certain you place their contact information on a special clients-only list. This is a great way of targeting previous buyers and offering them special deals.

Putting It All Together

The next step shouldn't be a surprise to anyone. We are going to take all three of the products in the previous chapters and offer them in a single email. Even better, we will offer the products to buy either a la carte or as a package deal.

The trick is to make the package deal the most appealing to the client. You can offer them 2 Yelp reviews, 2 video testimonials and 300 Facebook "likes" for $150, for example. If Yelp reviews cost $20 each, and video testimonials are $50 each, and you offer 100 Facebook "likes" for $50, suddenly the package deal looks fantastic.

I particularly love to play up the savings, advertising things like "this package will get you 20% off the normal price". It is unbelievably effective. And then once you outsource all the work for, say, $25 on Fiverr, you are left with a profit of $125. That's not a bad day's work. With a large enough client list, making thousands of dollars a day is easily within reach even with a low response rate. And as you build up a client list and get repeat customers, your profit can grow and grow.

Taking It to the Next Step

For those who feel comfortable setting up a website, you can always set up a social marketing company website where your potential customers can go. This doesn't have to be a full blown site, it can be as simple as a landing or squeeze page which explains more about your services and attempts to collect more information from the potential client.

If you do have a squeeze page, you can always advertise it on classified sites or even on business related bulletin boards in your signature. Anywhere business owners may be is a great place to mine. Since this is about using Fiverr to make money, I don't want to get too involved in this topic. If you are interested, you can always read an online marketing book which will give you tons of great ideas on how to promote your page.

What Is Good for your Client Is Good for You

Also, don't be shy to use the social media tools that I have given to you, particularly the social media exchange. You can create your social marketing site a Facebook page or a Twitter or Youtube account and get it all the followers and "likes" you want by utilizing the techniques in the previous chapters. This can also be quite helpful if any of your potential clients would like to see an example of your services. It gives you a great amount of social proof.

Using Fiverr to Make Passive Income

The last thing I want to cover is how to use Fiverr to create content that can make you a continuous passive income. There are two areas in which you can get a seller to create content for you that you can repackage and sell passively.

Taking Advantage of a Huge Market

We know that we can get reviews written on Fiverr, but this is only the tip of the iceberg when it comes to writing jobs available on Fiverr. There are many Fiverr sellers offering to write keyword dense content for you for five dollars. Here is how we take advantage of this and turn it into content we can sell.

Electronic books are a huge market online, particularly on Amazon. Now you may think that you need a novel of tens of thousands of words to sell, right? That couldn't be further from the truth. There is a huge market for shorter (think 3000 words or more) non-fiction books. This is the market we want to take advantage of.

We want to decide on a topic, for example, how to lose weight on a low carb diet. We then go to Fiverr and message a seller how much it would cost to get them to write six articles of at least 500 words on this topic. It is pretty easy to find a seller who will do this for around $25. We then package these articles up as an e-book and list it on the Kindle store. Voila, passive income.

There is a whole lot more to Kindle publishing than this, but this is the general idea of how to use Fiverr to create content that can be repackaged and sold elsewhere. If you are interested in publishing Kindle books, I recommend checking out my book, "Kindle Publishing Secrets Revealed", which is an in-depth, step-by-step guide that will teach you how to make money publishing Kindle books.

Getting to the Art of the Matter

Here is another area that you can use to create passive income: illustration. In particular, you want to buy vector illustrations from Fiverr sellers and then repackage them as prints, t-shirts, coffee mugs, and another else that can be printed on.

Here is what you do. I will use Cafepress (http://www.cafepress.com) as an example, but there are other similar sites out there which you can also use. Cafepress allows you to upload your design and then have that design available on a wide array of physical products. Once you upload the design, Cafepress takes care of the rest, including selling, producing, and shipping the products. And you get to collect the check.

This is a fantastic way to earn passive income since you have to do nothing more than commission a design on Fiverr and upload it and decide what products you want your design to appear on at a site like Cafepress.

While both of these methods require an upfront investment, they technically can generate an income for you for years, never requiring any maintenance or updating. It doesn't get much better than that.

Go Forth and Conquer

By employing the tools and techniques that I have taught you in this book, I have no doubt that you will find success.

Also, don't be afraid to add your own twist to your services. New Fiverr gigs are appearing every day, each a potential opportunity to sell more to your business contacts. Always keep an eye on your purpose: to buy services cheaply on Fiverr and sell them for much more to your customer base. With this in mind, you will be shocked with how quickly your bank account can grow.

Good luck, and happy Fiverring!

Kindle Publishing Secrets Revealed

How Selling E-Books Allowed Me to Quit My Job and Work Only Four Hours a Week

James Chen

Kindle Publishing Secrets Revealed © Copyright 2014 by James Chen. All rights reserved.

First Edition: May 2014
123456789
Published by Gamma Mouse http://gammamouse.com

This document is geared towards providing exact and reliable information in regards to the topic and issue covered. The publication is sold with the idea that the publisher is not required to render accounting, officially permitted, or otherwise, qualified services. If advice is necessary, legal or professional, a practiced individual in the profession should be ordered.

From a Declaration of Principles which was accepted and approved equally by a Committee of the American Bar Association and a Committee of Publishers and Associations.

In no way is it legal to reproduce, duplicate, or transmit any part of this document in either electronic means or in printed format. Recording of this publication is strictly prohibited and any storage of this document is not allowed unless with written permission from the publisher. All rights reserved.

The information provided herein is stated to be truthful and consistent, in that any liability, in terms of inattention or otherwise, by any usage or abuse of any policies, processes, or directions contained within is the solitary and utter responsibility of the recipient reader. Under no circumstances will any legal responsibility or blame be held against the publisher for any reparation, damages, or monetary loss due to the information herein, either directly or indirectly.

Respective authors own all copyrights not held by the publisher.

The information herein is offered for informational purposes solely, and is universal as so. The presentation of the information is without contract or any type of guarantee assurance.

The trademarks that are used are without any consent, and the publication of the trademark is without permission or backing by the trademark owner. All trademarks and brands within this book are for clarifying purposes only and are the owned by the owners themselves, not affiliated with this document.

Learn to Make Money with Kindle Books

Passive income. We all want to make it. And publishing books on Amazon Kindle is a great way to do it. Imagine your books earning money 24 hours a day, 365 days a year on autopilot, leaving you the time to do whatever you desire. Sounds like a wonderful life, right?

It can be, and the first step is publishing your book. This book will guide you step by step through the process, from initial research to how to market your book.

Don't think you are a very good writer? I will show you how outsource your ideas to other writers who will write the books for you. All you need to do is publish them. And collect the checks.

I will also divulge a secret niche which sees extraordinary sales and searches on Amazon. There are very few writers taking advantage of this trick, and those who have are seeing their books in the bestseller lists. The best part: this niche only requires the books be between 15 to 30 pages in length. Short books, huge rewards.

Learn to take advantage of Amazon's enormous customer base, publishing books that will be searched for, found, and purchased. Learn to get your books to stand out from the millions of other ones already available in the Kindle store. It is simple: if people cannot find your books, they will not buy them. Learn how to be found.

The #1 Rule of Kindle Marketing

The rule is simple: find a process that makes money. And repeat it. Over and over again. This rule is particularly effective in terms of Kindle publishing. You publish your book, market it, let it make money, and do the entire process again.

Too many writers concentrate on one book. They invest all of their energy in making it perfect, trying to build up and audience, instead of writing additional books. Understand that having one book found within millions of books requires a whole lot of luck. But if you have two books, your odds increase. Think of each book as a lottery ticket, the more you have, the more likely you will have one hit the jackpot. Your goal should not be to have one book in the Kindle store, but hundreds. Don't imagine yourself as a writer, but as a publisher. And act accordingly.

Authors often focus on the visible success stories on Amazon, on the fiction writers who have sold hundreds of thousands of books. This is an incredibly small group, and their success is hard to replicate, because it was brought about by luck. You will most likely never get this lucky, so you need to create your own success. That means publishing a lot of books.

The people making money in the system are those who publish hundreds of books under different pen names. These books are often outsourced to a group of writers, as are the formatting and cover creation. This book encourages you to embrace the second method and act like a publisher, producing and selling as much content as you can.

Remember the more you publish, the larger your slice of the pie will be.

Fiction or Non-Fiction?

Here's my problem with writing fiction books: too many are being given away for free. Customers start to expect it, they become conditioned to getting free books. It then becomes difficult to sell to them, especially if the book is priced higher than 99 cents.

Non-fiction books are generally viewed differently. They are informative, and customers still believe that you need to pay for information. This is why the majority of books that I publish are non-fiction; I am able to charge a higher price for them.

You will learn that you want to price books in the Amazon sweet spot, which is between $2.99 and $9.99. Within this range, you will earn a 70% royalty; outside this range you only get 35%. The difference is royalties is considerable. For example, if you sell a hundred copies of a 99 cent book at 35% royalty, you will earn $35. But if you sell the same hundred books at $2.99 and a 70% royalty, you will earn about $205. Using the lower pricing point and 35% royalty ends up leaving a lot of money on the table that you could otherwise be pocketing.

But don't you sell more books at 99 cents? Yes. But you have to sell over 5 books at 99 cents to match the royalty earned on the same book priced at $2.99. And in my experience, this rarely happens.

Trying to publish a fiction book priced at $2.99 is a difficult task for a new writer without an established audience. The competition is just too fierce, and one romance novel isn't really that different from another.

Non-fiction books are much more specific, often focusing on a certain idea or concept. When a customer searches Amazon for this topic, we want our book to come up at the top of the search results. Assume your book is about making money online. Now, assume a customer searches for this term on Amazon. Your book comes up. The chances are very high they will click on your book, because it addresses the issue they were searching for. Contrast this with a customer searching for a romance novel. A whole list will come up, all of the books hard to differentiate, because romance novels are highly similar to each other.

The obvious point is that non-fiction is more easily targeted to its audience. There is less selling involved.

People have a problem, search to fix that problem, find a book that promises to fix that problem, and then buy that book. This is the reason why this book will focus on publishing non-fiction material. You will find it to be the easy field in which to make money.

You can still publish fiction books if you wish, I have quite a few. But understand that you will make more if you concentrate on non-fiction books. And we are in this to make money on Amazon.

Researching Your Book

Now that we have decided on publishing a non-fiction book, it is time to select a topic. Often the best place to start is with subject matter that you are familiar with. If you have expertise in a certain area and are open to writing the book yourself, you can always write in that area.

Don't be daunted by the task of writing; this is not a full length book that we are talking about. Instead, we want short guides within the range of 3000 to 10000 words. Most of my books are in the 5000 word range, which translates to about 30 pages of content. If there is a subject you are interested in and believe you can write at least 3000 words, I encourage you to do it. Writing your own book will save you money, and you may find that you enjoy the creative process.

But will it sell? This is a huge question and is where research comes in. The easiest way to find out what people are searching for on Amazon is to check out the auto-fill selections when you start to type in Amazon's search box. For example, if I type "how to", I get the following search suggestions:

"how to win friends"

"how to draw"

"how to write a book"

"how to stop worrying"

You then keep drilling down on these suggestions, offering up new search terms until you find one you wish to pursue.

Another method is to use the categories list on the sidebar in the Kindle Store. Searching by category is a great way to see different topic areas that are available to you.

Keep your topic selection related to solving problems, like weight loss or dating advice. Any topic that gives people advice is generally good, because customers are searching for this information. You are providing them with a service by giving them what they want. And this is the best way to understand what type of topic you should pick: are you giving the customer what they want? If yes, it is definitely a topic you should select.

Make certain to write down your topic keyword. Use the Amazon search suggestion feature to find other phrases used by customers that are related to your keyword. Write all of these phrases down. They are very important. You will eventually use them as your keywords when you publish your book. For example, maybe your main keyword is "cookie recipes". Related keywords might be "how to bake cookies", "dessert recipes", "cookie cookbook", and so forth.

You want to make certain that you have at least seven keyword phrases. These need to be things that people are actually searching for on Amazon. The better your keywords, the more search results your book will show up in, and the more customers your book will get.

The Perfect Title

You've come up with the perfect niche, you have at least seven keywords, now all you need is a title, one that will really sell your book. In non-fiction, the best titles are one that align well with the term the customer searches for.

So for example, if you are targeting customers who are searching for "how to lose weight", not surprisingly, the best title for a book would be "How to Lose Weight".

Using the keyword in your title has another enormous benefit, it will put you higher up in the search results. The same is true for using the keyword in the book description that appears on Amazon's page.

Don't get too creative with your title, the simple ones work the best. While you may think having a keyword for a title is boring, the payoff in search results and sales make it worth it. A lot of writers think they have hit upon the perfect title only to discover that no one is searching for that. And if no one is searching for your book, no one is buying it.

Remember that you are giving your customers what they want. If they want to learn how to lose weight, it is your goal to give them a book telling them how to achieve success. And to make that goal obvious from just reading the title. Your title needs to mirror what the customer wants, and using your keyword in the title is the best way to guarantee this.

A subtitle is also needed for your book. I always incorporate at least one other related keyword into my subtitle. For example, "weight loss" is a related keyword to "how to lose weight", so if I title my book "How to Lose Weight", I might give it a subtitle like "Weight Loss Made Simple". The point is simple: use as many keywords as possible to have your book appear in the widest range of search results. The more results your book appears in, the better the chance you have at making a sale.

If you follow these steps in finding a niche and keyword and basing your title and subtitle on your keyword research, you have taken the first important step in publishing a Kindle book that sells. Understand that they are many good books on Amazon that don't sell. Just as there are many bad books that sell a lot of copies. The difference: the bad books appear for terms that customers are searching for, while the good books remain buried deep within the results. If no one sees your book, I don't care how good it is, it will never sell.

Writing Your Book

Once you have a title, and an idea of what your book is going to be about, you can set about the task of writing it. Or—if you don't want to write it—have the book written for you by a freelancer.

Even if you decide to write your first book, I recommend that you become acquainted with outsourcing this type of writing work. Eventually as success comes, you will want to produce more and more books. You won't be able to write them all, that would take too long. So outsourcing and hiring freelancers becomes the only alternative.

Another benefit of outsourcing your book is that you can concentrate on marketing and selling your books. Remember that the goal is to be a best-selling author and not necessarily the best-writing one. There is only so much time available, so it is necessary to be efficient in how you utilize it.

Besides I can outsource a 5000 word book for $20. The time it would take me to write a book of that length is worth more than $20. Make certain that you value your time properly. If you enjoy writing, that's fine, just understand that at some point if you really want to increase your Kindle publishing empire, you will need to outsource work.

There are quite a few websites where you can outsource your writing jobs, but I'm only going to cover the three major ones, Fiverr, Odesk, and Elance.

Fiverr (http://www.fiverr.com) is the largest marketplace of sellers who will do a variety of different jobs, called gigs, for five dollars. Writing jobs are just a small slice of what you can find on Fiverr. In fact, we will also use Fiverr to have a graphic artist design the cover for our book.

If you go to the Writing and Translation section on Fiverr, you will see a slew of individuals offering to write a certain amount of words for five dollars. The way I do it is to go through the gigs, read the descriptions, and eliminate the ones who don't have a polished description. I will then contact the individuals on my short list and ask if they would be willing to tackle a larger project of 3000 or more words. And if so, what would the price be. Not all of the sellers will be interested, but you will find a few. I then pick the one who I feel can do the best job on my book. Usually I will ask if they feel comfortable researching and writing about the subject matter I decided to write about. Don't hesitate to ask questions, and pay attention to the responses, particularly to the writing. Is it good? Do you want this person to write your book? If you treat this process like a job interview, you will most likely come away with the best candidate.

The biggest plus of Fiverr is that the majority of sellers have English as their first language. You will not be outsourcing to someone who might not have the strongest grasp on English grammar. Now, this isn't to say that all the writers on Fiverr are good. That is far from the case. But there are some very good ones there, you just need to search for them. And when you find a seller who does a good job, reward them with more projects. Publishing a lot of Kindle books requires you to establish good business relationships with as many contractors as you possible can.

Now what should you pay? No more than $50. In fact, I don't like to pay more than $40 for a book to be written. The reason is simple: I don't want to have to wait too long for the book to turn a profit after earning its cost back. On Fiverr, it will likely cost you $40 to $50 to get a book written. That's okay, particularly since it is written by a native English speaker. To get anything cheaper, you will need to outsource the work to residents of another country. And the best site for this is Odesk.

Odesk (http://www.odesk.com) is very similar to Fiverr in terms of the different categories of services being offered. The biggest difference is that it is a job posting site. You will post your job for a writer and people will apply for it. Sounds easy, right? It is, as long as you follow a few basic steps.

Job posting is easy, but you want to make certain that you are clear on what you expect in your job description. Tell them that you need a writer for a non-fiction book which needs to be between 3000 and 10000 words. Odesk allows you to set a fixed price for the job, and I recommend that you do. You will get responses if you set the budget at $20, but the higher you raise the price the better your responses will be. Most contractors apply within the first day with a cover letter and how much they are willing to accept to do the job. The screening and interview process is by far the most important, so these are the tips that I use to weed out the pretenders from the contenders.

Because you will get non-native English speakers applying for your job, you will want to screen them much more carefully. I always ask to see samples of their writing. I also ask a lot of questions, because I want to see how they respond. This is what you have to look out for: they show you beautifully written samples, but their messages to you don't show the same level of writing skill. These individuals you want to avoid as they are likely going to plagiarize the content they give to you. Some will just change words here and there and try to pass it off to you as original. Be very careful and vet your writers thoroughly.

If the contractor writes very good English in their answers to you, this is the type of person you want to hire. There are some very good non-native English writers on Odesk, but it definitely takes work to find them.

Now this doesn't make Odesk sound great, so why would we use it? The price. I can often get a 5000 word book written for $25. It won't necessarily be the best quality, but it will be more than good enough. Personally, I get the majority of my books written by contractors on Odesk. There are a few who always do a great job for me, so I tend to keep them busy. Once again, it is about building business relationships; if you find someone good, hang on to them and keep them working.

Elance (http://www.elance.com) is a job posting site similar to Odesk, but with more contractors based in the United States and Canada. It is a good second option if Odesk doesn't work out for you. Elance also lets you set a budget on your job postings, and I recommend that you do it. You will get a large variety of applicants, many of them quite good. And also quite expensive. It isn't unusual to have a contractor quote hundreds of dollars to write a 5000 word book.

And this is the greatest issue with using Elance. It just costs too much. You don't want to have to sell hundreds of copies of the book just to break even. You want to make money, and spending too much money on producing your books is a sure way not to see a profit for a while.

Understand that your goal should be to get the best quality books written for the cheapest price possible. Produce your titles cheaply. It requires some work to find people who can produce quality content for a cheap price, but this is a task you only have to do once. Once you find enough contractors to create all your content, producing books becomes an extremely simplified process. And this is why cultivating these business relationships with your best contractors is vitally important. Their work will build your publishing business.

Creating the Perfect Cover

You know the saying don't judge a book by its cover? Forget about it. Amazon shoppers clearly do. A great cover can sell a terrible book. But a terrible cover won't sell your book no matter how good it may be. So you need a cover that pops.

Fortunately, this isn't as difficult as it sounds. What it boils down to is that you want the keyword that you are focusing on to be readable when it shows up in the Amazon search results. This means that the title needs to be clear and visible to the customer. If you have that with a clean, professional look, your book will sell. Guaranteed.

Remember that you are giving your customers what they really want. And what they really want is answers. If a book's cover promises this in big, bold letters that will be attractive to them. It will be the solution that they are searching for.

While you can use either Elance or Odesk to hire a graphic artist to design your book cover, I don't recommend that. It will end up costing you more than you need to spend. Instead, we will use Fiverr.

Go to Fiverr and do a search for "book covers". The search should return a bunch of gigs. You may see both 3D and regular book covers offered; you definitely want to purchase a 2D flat regular book cover. I suggest taking the time and going through the various gigs, looking through each artist's portfolio. Find someone who you feel can match your vision for the cover.

You don't need to pay more than $5 for a cover; you don't need any of the fancy extras like the original file formats. When you contact the seller, you want to make certain that you specify that the cover is for a "Kindle book". Amazon has size requirements for the cover, the largest size has to be a minimum of 1000 pixels. The majority of Fiverr cover designers know this, so they will size your book cover appropriately if you tell them this information.

A word of advice. I went through quite a few cover designers on Fiverr until I found one who produce the kind of covers that I was looking for. If you can, it may be a good idea to hire a few designers to design your cover and pick the best one. Since each gig only costs $5 a pop, it is not too great of an investment. And the payoff of finding a really good designer will make it totally worth it in the long run.

Preparing Your Book

Your contractor has finished writing your book and has sent you the Word document. Now what?

I suggest reading over the document, checking for errors and spelling mistakes. With spell check this should be a relatively easy process. You will also want to insert a title page at the beginning of the document. On this title page, you should put the title, the subtitle, and the author's name. Keep it simple; there is no reason not to.

After the title page is where I normally put my copyright page. This could be as simple as writing "Copyright (Insert Year) by (Author's Name or Publisher's Name)". It isn't a problem if you don't have it, but it does add to the professionalism of your book.

A table of contents is another nice touch to add. In Word, you can go to the References tab, select the Table of Contents drop-down menu, and then select Custom Table of Contents. This will open up a dialog box. You want to make sure that you uncheck "Show page numbers" before hitting OK. The table of contents will then auto-generate itself using the headings of each of the chapters. If the headings are not showing up, check that the chapter titles are actually in the "Heading 1" style. If not, change them and re-generate your table of contents.

Once I have a few published books in my library, I like to place previews of these books at the end of my newest books. Usually I will have the first chapter as a preview. Think of this as the perfect opportunity to sell your reader on more of your books. I often put two free previews at the back of my book, as well as a listing of all of my titles with clickable Amazon links.

Once the title page and any extras you desire have been added, it is time to convert the document to a format that can be upload to Kindle Direct Publishing. The first step is to save your Word document as a "Web Page, Filtered".

The next step is to download and install the Kindle Previewer:

http://www.amazon.com/gp/feature.html?docId=1000765261

Start the Kindle Previewer and load your manuscript in the Web Page, Filtered format. The Kindle Previewer will automatically convert your book into the needed format. It is that simple. It will also give you the opportunity to see how your book will look on a Kindle. Go through it quickly to make certain you don't have any glaring formatting issues.

You now have everything you need to publish your book in the Kindle Store.

Publishing Your Book

If you haven't set up an account on Amazon's Kindle Direct Publishing, you need to do that now. Go to http://kdp.amazon.com to sign up. Once you sign up, you will be given access to your bookshelf. Since you have not published any books yet, it will be empty.

Since we are adding a new book, we want to click on the "Add new title" button. On the first page, you will enter your book's details. The first box asks if you want to enroll your book in KDP Select, check yes. This allows your book to be borrowed by Amazon Prime members. The best part: you will get paid for it. It is a great source of additional revenue.

Next, enter your book title and subtitle that you determined as part of your initial research. Unless the book is part of a series, leave the next box unchecked. I usually leave the edition number and publisher boxes blank, but it really is up to you. There is no benefit one way or the other.

The description is very important. You want to take your time here. This is the where you want to really sell your book. Focus on your keywords and make certain that they are in your description. Try to write as much as possible; you don't want short descriptions. I've noticed that my books that have the longer descriptions seem to sell better than books with shorter descriptions. Don't worry about the description being perfect, you can always change and revise it later if necessary after the book is published.

Next, add the contributors to your book. I suggest using a pen name. If you publish enough books, you will want a separate pen name for each genre. Always remember that when customers search for your pen name, all your books will appear. If they are related, the chances of an additional sale increase. If they are not related, you may lose credibility in the eyes of that customer.

Indicate your book's language and publication date, if you wish. You can ignore the ISBN box unless you have one; you don't need one, though. Under the Verifying Your Publishing Rights, you will want to select "This is not a public domain work and I hold the necessary publishing rights."

Selecting categories is another important step that you want to take your time with. Here is my suggestion: search the Kindle Store for your main keyword. Click on the first book in the search results. Go down to the book's details. You will see a ranking in the paid Kindle Store. Underneath this ranking, you might see additional rankings on the bestseller lists in various categories. If that is the case, note these categories and use them with your book. If the book doesn't have these rankings, keep searching the results until you find a book that does.

You want to select a category that does not have a lot of competition for the bestseller lists. Getting on the bestseller lists is the key for increasing your book's visibility. The good news is that you can tweak this until you find a related category that you can get listed on with little competition.

In the next box, enter the seven keywords that you uncovered in your research. Now, upload the cover that you outsourced as well as the book file that you produced using the Kindle Previewer. Do not worry about digital rights management; if people are going to pirate your book, digital rights management won't stop them. After you have uploaded both your cover and book, click Save and Continue to go to the pricing page.

The pricing page is much simpler, only requiring a few pieces of information. You want to check 70% royalty and enter a price of $2.99 in the box for the Amazon.com store. The other stories will automatically calculate their price in their currency based on the Amazon.com price.

I suggest checking the box that allows users to lend their book to others; it doesn't hurt and it allows you to build your potential audience. Once you agree to Amazon's terms and conditions, you can then proceed to publish your book. It takes approximately 12 hours for your book to become available in the Kindle store.

Congratulations! You have just published your first Kindle book. To check your sales, you can go to the Reports tab on the Kindle Direct Publishing website.

Getting Reviews

Positive reviews are definitely important in selling your book. They offer social proof; customers will often pick a book with a hundred positive reviews over one with only a few reviews.

While reviews are important to the success of your book, they are not nearly as important as some authors seem to believe. I have many books that had no reviews sell much better than books with quite a few reviews; reaching a certain audience will sell more books than reviews often will.

The point is not to stress out about reviews. Particularly bad reviews. There will come, and it is easier to ignore them than to get worked up about them. The hardest part about reviews is getting them.

Most new authors have no idea how difficult it is to get reviews of their work. They figure that if they sell a few books, or offer a free promotion, the reviews will pour in. This is far from the truth. Reviews are rare. You might have to have a thousand people download your book for free to get even one review. And that is far from guaranteed. Most of the people who buy or download your book will not take the time to review it.

That can't be right, you say. You see books with lots of reviews on Amazon. How do they get their reviews?

And this is where the dirty little secret in Amazon's review system is uncovered. A huge amount of the book reviews you see in the Kindle Store for self-published books are either by friends or family members or were purchased. Most of the self-published authors who have been successful on Amazon like John Locke have bought reviews. A lot of reviews.

It is important to understand that fake reviews is truly how the system works. That's not to say that real reviews don't happen, just that they are rare. Understand that this is more an issue with self-published books. The traditionally published books have a larger audience base, with many who actually do review books. Indie authors don't have this luxury.

So this leaves you with a decision: do you wait for reviews to appear organically or do you purchase reviews for your books? If you decide to purchase reviews, you can go on Fiverr and search for "book reviews". There are many sellers offering positive reviews for $5.

If you do purchase reviews, you want to make certain you buy a verified review. A verified review is one in which the reviewer purchases your book and posts a review. Verified reviews carry a heavier weight when Amazon calculates their search results. The easiest and most cost effective way to get verified reviews is to purchase your reviews during one of your books free promotions.

Understand that purchasing reviews or soliciting reviews from friends or family is against Amazon's guidelines. Amazon has the right to remove the review if they think it is suspect. Furthermore, reviewing another author's work in exchange for them reviewing yours is also against the guidelines. It is important that you are aware of this in making your choice.

Because of the inflated review system, you want to make certain that your book has at least an average of

4 stars. Anything less will likely impact your sales. If you are finding that you are getting bad reviews, you will want to think about having your book revised to increase its quality. Another option is to purchase five star reviews which will raise your book's average.

What it comes down to with getting reviews is deciding whether you want to purchase reviews or not. It is a question of ethics. Realize that your competition is likely buying reviews, so waiting for reviews to appear organically for your book will likely see you losing ground and potential customers.

The Perfect Niche

This chapter is going to introduce you to one of the most profitable niches for Kindle books on Amazon. This isn't a regular niche, but rather a very specialized type of book. These books sell incredibly well, because they piggyback on the notoriety of other books.

Remember when you were in school and your English teacher would assign a book for a book report. If you were like me, you probably didn't read the book. Instead, you used one of the various Notes's guides that summarized and analyzed the book. This audience still exists to this day; they have just grown up.

This is the demand that you will satisfy. And you will do it by basically writing book reports of current non-fiction or fiction bestsellers.

Let me explain. A customer searches for the newest hot book on Amazon, the search results return the book as well as your summary book. Often the customer will notice the price difference between the two. The regular book is likely over ten dollars, while your book is less than 5. This alone gets them to click on your book. Your summary book piggybacks on the popularity of the regular book.

So what should our summary involve? Imagine you are writing a book report, summarize the chapters, detail the characters, and add your own thoughts. Make it at least 3000 words, and you have just created a bestselling Kindle book.

If the name of the book you are making a reader's guide for is "Title X", you want to title your book "Title X Reader's Guide". Add a subtitle like "A Summary and Analysis." It is important that you don't hide the fact that your book is a reader's guide. Make certain that information is prominent, because you don't want to fool people, you just want to offer them a less expensive, cheaper alternative.

Publishing reader's guides for popular books is very lucrative. Particularly because the audience is huge. It's not unusual for these reader's guides to make $20 or more a day during the height of a book's popularity. Just imagine you had ten of these reader's guides and were pocketing $200 a day. Not bad, right?

There is a drawback, though. Reader's guides tend to earn big profits up front, but earn less and less as the book they are based on starts to wan in popularity. This means that you have to constantly put out new guides for other books to maintain a steady stream of income.

Diversification is key to using this method. You want to publish books as outlined in this guide that will be steady earners. You can then supplement these with reader's guides. The combination of the two can bring tremendous monetary rewards to you.

If you decide to publish a reader's guide, follow the steps as outlined in this book. Everything works the same, the title of your book will just tap into a much larger market.

Another trick to tap into a popular book's audience is to give one of your books the same title, but a different subtitle. You do need to be careful not to try and pass yourself off as the book; it is generally safer to be in a different genre, or to have a clearly distinguishable difference in subject matter.

I have seen this tactic employed a few times, and it has never failed in raising the sales rank of the book that is cashing in on the more popular book's title. And it isn't because you are fooling people, it is because you are reaching a much larger search audience. The point is to get your book in front of as many customers as possible. The more customers who view your book, the more who will eventually buy it.

Marketing Your Book

How to market your Kindle book is a broad topic. Many books could be written on this subject. The method outlined in this guide doesn't rely heavily on marketing, so I'm only going to cover a few tips that will be helpful.

After publishing your book, you will want to set up a free promotion of it for a day. This is a great way to get your book moving in the system. When you enroll in Kindle Select you are allowed to give your book away for free for a total of five days. You can take all the days at once, or space them out of the course of 90 days.

Never run a free promotion for more than a day; you want to sell the book, not give it away. If you are buying reviews for your book, you want to schedule them to coincide with your free promotion so you can get the verified option.

There are quite a few sites that will promote your free book if you submit the information. Most of them need you to submit the information days in advance. This will definitely get you more downloads and a higher ranking in the Free Kindle Store, which increases your exposure even more.

You can also write up a press release for your book (or hire someone on Fiverr to do it) and submit it to press release sites. The benefit of this is that your press release may eventually find itself indexed by search engines. This potentially allows more customers to eventually find your book.

Just as there are sites that promote free Kindle books, there are many that promote 99 cent books. If you want to jumpstart your sales, you can lower your price to 99 cents for a limited time and promote it on these sites. This is essentially a short term solution only, and not particularly effective.

Another option is to have a seller on Fiverr create a book trailer for your book, and then you can post it to Youtube. This is a great way to get indexed into the search engines. Want to get more views and likes to your video, use social media exchange site like http://www.like4like.org. These sites allow you to build up credits by liking other pages, and then spending those credits on having people view and like your page. It is a great way to increase the popularity of your social media page quickly.

You can also use this technique with Facebook pages and Twitter accounts. One effective use is to run your free promotion, tweet about it, and then use a social media exchange to get your message retweeted. I've been able to achieve some amazing reach employing this technique.

Your marketing should be entirely focused on building up your audience. That way when you do make an announcement, it will have the greatest impact. You don't have time to build your audience personally, responding to every tweet. You need to be able to build your audience fast and with little effort.

Final Word

You are now ready to tackle the wonderful world of Kindle publishing. All the tools you need to be successful have been given to you. The trick is keep publishing more and more books, always giving yourself a better chance to sell more books.

The tip alone on the lucrative nature of reader's guides should give you a great head start if you choose to go that route. Never forget that luck plays a large role in whether a book is successful or not. But here is the good news: you can make your own luck. Following the suggestions in this guide is gives you the best chance to ultimate succeed as a Kindle book publisher.

Good luck. And happy publishing.

Preview of "Cellulite Reduction: The Ultimate Guide on How to Get Rid of Cellulite" by Emily V. Steinhauser

What is cellulite in the first place?

As mentioned, cellulite is normal fat or may also be additional fat that is found underneath the connective layers of the skin. The unsightly lines and furrows on the skin develop as the fat pushes against the skin.

Cellulite is more common in women than in men simply because females have more fat tissue compared to their male counterparts. This is because of the difference of fat distribution in a woman's body compared to men. Cellulite may also be present no matter what body type you are which means even thin people have it. Finally, having cellulite does not mean that you are fat it's just that your body is more prone to develop it than other people.

Interesting cellulite facts:

If your parents and other family members have cellulite there is a huge possibility that you will also develop cellulite too.

There are so many reasons why a person develops cellulite, in women; hormones may play a huge role.

You can hardly see cellulite in people with dark skin color but it is still there.

Liposuction is one of the oldest but still effective ways to remove fatty layers on skin however the American Academy of Dermatology cautions about liposuction. They say that it only worsen the appearance of cellulite since the procedure may only create additional depressions on skin.

The best way to remove cellulite is careful planning. This involves a combination of the right diet, exercise, lifestyle changes and the use of effective treatments.

Prevention may help reduce the development of cellulite and prevention also includes diet, exercise and lifestyle changes.

Your dermatologist and your doctor are the best sources of information regarding the removal of cellulite.

What are the signs of cellulite?

First of all you need to spot cellulite to be able to plan how to get rid of it. The common places that you can find cellulite are parts of the body where excess fat usually deposit. Thus you may find cellulite on the thighs, the hips, buttocks, upper arms, on the midsection and sometimes on the neck area. Skin may appear

- Dimpled and uneven
- With obvious irregular marks on the surface of the skin
- There is discoloration along the area especially when viewed under natural light

Knowing the signs of cellulite will help people develop the ideal cellulite removal plan. Since cellulite may be reduced, if not removed, with the use of exercise, the ideal exercise regimen to tone the area with cellulite may be done.

I hope you enjoyed this free preview of "Cellulite Reduction: The Ultimate Guide on How to Get Rid of Cellulite" by Emily V. Steinhauser.

Preview of "Texting Secrets Revealed" by Vin Petrillo

Chapter 1 – The Approach

What is the "Approach"? In a typical pickup scenario—say in a bar or nightclub—the approach refers to making first contact with your intended target. This usually means approaching them and striking up a conversation. Simply stated, there are a ton of theories about the most effective way to approach a woman.

If you struggle with this portion of your game, I suggest reading pickup books that deal with this topic. While each may give you specific techniques, the overall takeaway will be to improve your approaches you must practice. The more experience you get, the better.

This applies equally to text dating. Practice is essential. I've noticed on of the big differences between the two is shy guys feel more comfortable texting than a real-world approach. This highlights a problem which needs to be overcome if you wish to have success in attracting girls: being shy. Nothing ruins your chances more than being shy. If you want to be successful, you need to face your fears straight on.

Most people fear public speaking. They often feel like they are being judged; that any mistakes they make are a personal reflection. Approaching girls magnifies these feelings. It becomes extremely personal. But this is a mistake; it isn't personal. It is not a reflection on you. If a girl rejects your pickup attempt, understand that is snap judgment. She doesn't know you; she doesn't know what the correct decision. She can only make a snap decision. Don't confuse the two.

One of the best life lessons that I ever got was to learn to embrace failure. You have likely heard the quote: that which does not kill you, makes you stronger. It's true. Failure breeds strength.

Pretend you are stuck in a maze. You wander around trying to find the exit. Every dead end that you encounter guides you closer and closer to the exit. By making wrong turns, you are able to discover the one true path. Dating is similar. Making mistakes will lead you to the path of success.

If your heart pounds and your hands sweat on an approach, take a moment and examine the thoughts that are controlling these feelings of fear. Ask yourself: what is there to be afraid of? Failure? Now ask yourself: is failure a bad thing? Or could it be a good thing?

Imagine you approach an attractive girl in a bar and you blow it; you get rejected. That sucks, right? Obviously this girl is the greatest thing on two legs, right? You feel like getting rejected is a bad thing. Later on, you discover this girl has a serious drug problem; she is a flake and steals from the people closest to her. How do you feel now? Maybe like you dodged a big, fucking bullet.

Realize that keeping perspective is always important. Understand that on the approach both parties are working with imperfect information. Your hope is that hooking up with this hottie will be a good thing. Instead, it might be the most catastrophic event in your life. The same thing applies to her.

The point is to stop looking at your results in the light of good or bad. That just screws your emotions up. If you believe you lost something good, you will feel sad.

Just as if you lost something bad, you would likely feel relieved.

So don't automatically equate failure with bad. Just like taking the wrong path in a maze is not bad. It just lengthens your journey.

Having the right mental attitude is an aspect that most dating advice books avoid. They will tell you to practice your approaches, but never offer any advice on how to conquer any fears you have. To control your fears, you need to show yourself that they are unfounded. Do not let yourself be fooled by your thoughts. Getting rejected and failing—at anything—is not automatically a bad thing; it can be a good thing. Just like turning down the wrong path in a maze is not inherently bad. Making mistakes helps us find the correct path.

If you still find yourself struggling with approaching people, take an acting class at the local community college or through a university extension program. Acting is wonderful for strengthen your presence and verbal abilities. Some students find it incredibly helpful also, because pretending to be a character in a play makes a social situation like approaching a beautiful girl less daunting. At the very least, acting classes can help you fake it until you make it.

While this is not the type of approach meant in text dating, it is helpful advice in improving your ability to approach women. The benefit should be obvious. The more women you approach, the more numbers you get. And the more girls you can text. Simply stated, if you don't approach girls and get their numbers, you aren't going to have any one to text.

But what about the texting Approach, namely sending that first text? I will discuss the case in which you have never met the person previously. The rest of this book will discuss texting girls you already know (though all of it also works for girls you don't know yet, too).

Say you are looking to message a girl. You saw her profile online, maybe on a dating site or social media site, you think she is cute and want to get to know her. What should you message her?

Understand that getting responses in these types of situations can be difficult. One of the best ways that I have discovered to elicit a response is to act like you have information that she would want to know. One example of this is as follows: you message her, "I can't believe you put that on your profile. How did you not get banned?"

Most girls read this, and their curiosity gets the better of them. They are confused and want to know what you are talking about. They also don't want to have anything embarrassing on their profile. Most will message you back wanting to know what you are talking about.

Your reply should be short: "You are in the middle of meeting a deadline, and you will get back to her later." The point is not to have an answer, but to make initial contact. After this, wait a week and then contact her normally. Don't bring up your initial message; forget it. Let her bring it up if she remembers, then ignore it. Just plow ahead, run your game.

Making contact like this should be the rare case. Don't expect tremendous success employing this type of cold-reading messaging. If this is your entire game, you need to work on approaching girls and getting more numbers. Understand that cold-reading messaging is similar to a telemarketer calling random people; there is a low probability of success. On the plus side of these cold-reading approaches is that you can experiment a lot, trying a variety of ideas without much effort. I suggest typing up your script in Notepad and copying and pasting in message boxes. Realize that this is a machine gun approach to texting, you will eventually hit a target if you shoot enough bullets.

Now that I've talked a little about approaches, the rest of the book will examine the nitty-gritty of text dating.

I hope you enjoyed this free preview of "Texting Secrets Revealed" by Vin Petrillo.

Other Books Available From Gamma Mouse Media

Below you will find other popular Amazon bestsellers from Gamma Mouse Media.

25 Tips to Improve your Text Dating Game – Aidan Upton

Knee Pain Treatment – Emily V. Steinhauser

Quiet – Amelia Austin

Lust for Me – Amelia Austin

Text Dating Secrets Revealed – Vin Petrillo

Cellulite Reduction – Emily V. Steinhauser

The Quick Start Guide to Macarons – Lindsay Stotts

Speed Reading Training – Warren R. Sullivan

Memory Enhancement – Warren R. Sullivan

Text Dating – Vin Petrillo and Aidan Upton

The Quick Start Guide to Perfect Pancakes – Lindsay Stotts

Stormy Passions – Shad Gable

www.ingramcontent.com/pod-product-compliance
Lightning Source LLC
Chambersburg PA
CBHW072040190526
45165CB00018B/1186